# The Cyborg Age

## *How Bionic Implants Are Changing Lives*

# Table of Contents

# Chapter 1. Introduction

Welcome to a breathtaking journey into the dawn of a new era. In our special report, "The Cyborg Age: How Bionic Implants Are Changing Lives," we delve into an awe-inspiring world that straddles the junction of science fiction and reality. Advances in technology have brought us closer to an intriguing yet somewhat unsettling future where the lines between human and machine are becoming increasingly blurred. But fear not, this report grounds these high-tech concepts into relatable, everyday examples, humanizing the giants of technology and demonstrating the positive impact bionic implants are currently driving in the lives of millions around the globe. As you turn the pages, expect to be enlightened, surprised, and inspired by the stories of true transformation. Whether you're tech enthusiast or a curious newcomer, this special report promises to be a thought-provoking read that will leave you eager to explore the wonders of the inevitable Cyborg Age!

# Chapter 2. The Dawn of the Cyborg Age

In the early stages of civilization, the human body was considered sacrosanct, protected from any technological intervention. But as the human understanding of science and technology has grown, we've learned that the human body is not just a temple, but a canvas: a platform for improvement, refinement, and even evolution.

The universe of science fiction has long speculated the existence of 'cyborgs' – a blend of man and machine, resulting in beings that aren't quite human but also not merely robotic. But the dawn of the cyborg age isn't some distant dystopian future; it is the world we live in today.

## 2.1. The Evolution of Body Modification

Body modification dates back many thousands of years - from the simplest forms like hair dyeing and tattooing to more complex surgeries. Flash forward to the future we are currently experiencing, and body modification has taken on a new form – bionic implants. Bionic implants are artificial devices that replace or augment missing physiological structures to enhance humans' abilities, from correcting impairments to augmenting the 'normal' human experience. This opens up a wealth of opportunities for human augmentation.

## 2.2. Bionic Implants and Prosthetics

Typically, the first picture that comes to mind when we say 'bionic implants' is that of prosthetics. Prosthetics have come a long way from peg legs and hook hands. Now, they can replicate the appearance and function of an actual limb, thanks to the advent of myoelectric technology.

This technology relies on electromyogram (EMG) signals, which are the electrical signals our muscles produce when they move. Once the user thinks about moving their artificial limb, the sensors in the prosthetic pick up on these EMG signals and translate them into movements. Advanced variations of these prosthetics can even offer tactile feedback, enabling the wearer to feel pressure, texture, and temperature, just like a natural limb would.

## 2.3. Sensory Augmentation

Bionic implants don't stop at correcting physical impairments only. They're now used to enhance our sensory experiences as well. An excellent example of this are cochlear implants, which can provide a sense of sound to those with hearing impairments. Unlike hearing aids, which amplify sound, these implants bypass damaged areas of the ear and directly stimulate the auditory nerve. The user hears these nerve signals as sounds.

Further research is also underway to develop bionic eyes. For example, the Argus II, developed by Second Sight, is a retina prosthesis system that stimulates the retina's remaining cells to provide the sensation of sight. The technology, though in its early stages, offers a promising future for those affected by degenerative eye diseases.

## 2.4. The Road to Cognitive Enhancement

Imagine a future where bionic implants are used for cognitive enhancement. The concept may seem far-fetched, but certain strides have already been made in this direction. A prime example is Elon Musk's Neuralink - a neurotechnology company aiming to implant wireless brain-machine interfaces that could facilitate communication with computers.

Another instance is the work being done by a company named Kernel. They're pioneering the development of neuroprosthetics that can improve cognitive functions like intelligence, memory, and attention, potentially unlocking the secrets of the human brain and opening the door to unexplored possibilities of cognitive augmentation.

## 2.5. Ethical Considerations

The rapid advance of bionic technologies does, however, raise an array of ethical questions. Who gets to access these technologies? What does the advent of superhumans mean for society at large? How far can we push the boundaries of human evolution before we lose our humanity?

These are not easy questions to answer, and it's essential to have all stakeholders - from tech companies, end-users, ethicists, and society at large - at the table as we navigate the dawning cyborg age.

As we stand on the brink of a new era, it is time for us to ponder our place, as individuals and as a species, amidst the seismic shifts our technological empowerment is about to bring. With bionic technology, we hold the power to redefine what it means to be human. It's an exhilarating, daunting path, yet one we must tread with caution, curiosity, and an unwavering commitment to our collective humanity.

# Chapter 3. Understanding Bionic Implants: A Primer

To initiate this journey, it is critical to grasp the fundamental concept underlying it all: the bionic implant. Bionic implants, at their most basic, are devices engineered to replace or enhance organ functionalities. The realm of bionics is not bound by addressing health considerations alone. Instead, it transcends into spheres of cognitive augmentation and the enhancement of human capabilities beyond their biological limits.

## 3.1. What are Bionic Implants?

Simply put, a bionic implant is an artificial device that supplants or augments a part of the body riddled with malfunction or incapacitation. These devices function by interacting with the body's nervous system, muscles, or other biological interfaces.

The use of these implants encompasses a rather broad spectrum, from those we incorporate for medical necessities — like cochlear implants for hearing loss or heart pacemakers — to the more futuristic constructs involving cognitive ability enhancements.

## 3.2. The History of Bionic Implants

Understanding the progression of bionic implants over time offers a remarkable testament to human ingenuity.

These miraculous contraptions have their roots in the pacemaker, which was first invented in the late 1950s to control irregular heart rhythms. From those simpler beginnings, the field of bionics has advanced rapidly. It made strides towards developing artificial hearts, artificial eyes offering sensory perception, spinal cord stimulators to mitigate chronic pain, and mind-controlled prosthetics.

## 3.3. How Do Bionic Implants Work?

A common question is, how can a non-biological entity interpret signals from a biological system, and vice versa? The answer lies within the realm of bioengineering. Bionic implants work through interfaces that use nerve signals to control their functions.

For instance, consider a bionic arm. The user might flex certain muscles in their residual limb, which would, in turn, generate electrical signals. These signals are then detected by the bionic arm and translated into a specific movement—like opening a fist or rotating a wrist—using an in-built microprocessor.

## 3.4. The Science Behind Bionic Implants

One pivotal field that has fueled advances in bionics is biomaterials science. The materials used in bionic implants need to be biocompatible to ensure they don't harm the body nor have their functional properties degraded by the body's environment.

Materials such as titanium and silicone have long been the choice in most implants due to their durability, corrosion resistance, and minimal chance of rejection by the body. In the never-ending quest for perfection, scientists are now developing bioabsorbable electronics that dissolve harmlessly within the body after serving their purpose.

## 3.5. The Role of AI and Machine Learning

Artificial intelligence (AI) and machine learning have raised the bar in the field of bionics. They have helped create predictive models that allow for the refinement of system controls and improved adaptability of the devices based on user preferences.

One example is the increasing use of AI in prosthetics to improve the dexterity of artificial limbs. Machine learning algorithms are being trained on patterns of muscle activity to predict and execute complex movements, thus resulting in more intuitive control for the users.

## 3.6. Impact on Quality of Life

From restoring hearing to the hearing-impaired to providing independence to those who lost their limbs, bionic implants have undoubtedly improved millions of lives worldwide.

While medical necessity has been the driving force behind their adoption, an exciting prospect lies in enhancing human capabilities. Imagine recalling any information at will with a memory-enhancing implant, or a chip allowing us to perceive the vast spectrum of infra-red or UV light.

## 3.7. Ethical Considerations

As with all groundbreaking technologies, bionic implants come with their share of ethical and moral implications. Issues such as the affordability of these technologies, potential for enhancements to be used for disguise or deceit, or even the very idea of "playing God" need to be addressed.

While these discussions are beyond the scope of a primer, they're important to the development and application of these technologies and must not be dismissed.

As we continue our exploration into the Cyborg Age, keep in mind that while these may seem like concepts of the far-off future, they're absolutely within our reach in the very near future. The advances in bionics are closing the divide between the biological and mechanical, ushering us into an era where our limitations can be continually redefined by technological evolution.

As the journey through this awe-inspiring field unfurls, the line where human ends and machine begins will continue to blur.

# Chapter 4. The Intersection of Humanity and Technology

The first recorded attempt to replace or supplement human capabilities with technology goes back to ancient Egypt, where prosthetic toes were used to aid the afflicted in walking. These early efforts were primitive by today's standards, but they marked the beginning of a millennia-long quest to augment human abilities using technology. From the first spectacles in thirteenth-century Italy to modern prosthetics and hearing aids, mankind has striven to overcome its physical limitations.

The last century has seen tremendous advancements in this field, and we're now stepping into an age where technology fused with biology is no longer a marvel associated exclusively with high-tech laboratories or science fiction. The term 'cyborg' isn't alien to us, thanks to popular culture. However, the reality is far from an apocalyptic narrative. We're already living in the 'Cyborg Age,' where bionic implants have robustly impacted lives, making differences in ways mundane yet life-altering.

## 4.1. Digging Deeper Into Bionics

The term "bionics" was coined in the 1950s, derived from a combination of "biology" and "electronics." It describes an interdisciplinary field where biological systems inspire the development of artificial systems, ranging from computer programming to physical, mechanical devices. Early instances of bionics in practice involved part replacement or substitution, focusing primarily on restoring damaged body parts to a "normal" functionality.

However, modern bionics has taken a quantum leap from just replacement. The new focus is not just about reaching normalcy, but transcending to augmentation. It's about adding new capabilities that go beyond the limitations of our biology. Current biological research is going extraordinary lengths to synchronise technology with the human body to unravel undreamed possibilities.

## 4.2. Under the Skin - Implants

One of the significant breakthroughs resulting from this technological innovation is the development of bionic implants. They are devices inserted into or attached onto the body to replicate or augment a particular biological function.

The range of such implants is incredibly vast. If we look at sensory enhancements, you have the Cochlear implant, a unit that is surgically implanted into a person's head to provide a sense of sound to those with profound hearing loss. Once the preserve of profound deafness, it's now increasingly used in lesser hearing impairments, providing a significantly improved quality of life.

In the realm of mobility, consider the bionic limb innovations, giving amputees the chance to regain their independence. Advanced prosthetic limbs replicate the complex movements of natural limbs with such finesse that they can engage in activities otherwise impossible for an amputee, like climbing mountains or participating in marathons.

## 4.3. Towards Boundless Health - Bionic and Medicine

Medicine's intersection with bionics is bridging human limitations and former fatality sentences into new stories of survival. Bionic eyes offering visual discerning capabilities, bioartificial kidneys as an alternative to kidney transplants, or brain implants aiding Parkinson's patients show us how we're reinventing medical trajectories.

Recently, technologies such as deep brain stimulation (DBS) have revolutionised treatments for neurodegenerative disorders. These implants send electrical impulses to specific brain regions, thereby alleviating symptoms of diseases like Parkinson's, dystonia, or obsessive-compulsive disorder. It's a significant enhancement over pharmacotherapy, enabling a shift from symptomatic treatment to addressing root abnormalities.

## 4.4. Understanding the Intricacies

The development of these bionic implants is no cakewalk. It requires exhaustive and multidisciplinary research in biomedical engineering, neuroscience, computer science, and material science. Key challenges to implant development often revolve around designing systems that can seamlessly link electronic components with the biological world, establishing long-term compatibility.

The implants should resist tissue rejection, need to be durable, and importantly, operate without causing discomfort. Plus, they must replicate the assigned function using a meager power source, since impractical to have them powered from an external source.

## 4.5. A New Era of Interaction

Beyond the implants, the surrounding components of the system also play a crucial role. User interfaces must be intuitive and unobtrusive. For instance, someone using a bionic arm should feel the movement as naturally as moving a biological limb. Telemetry and control systems are also essential, controlling the implant and retrieving valuable data that can assist in further refining its functioning.

# 4.6. Future Directions

Looking ahead, the momentum in bionics research is towards refinement, improving the interface between the implant and the body to enhance acceptance and performance. Eventually, this could blur the perceptible differences between a biological limb and its bionic counterpart. Future bionic implants may also feature adaptive learning, progressing from need-based responses to real-time adjustments based on the user's behaviour and environment.

In conclusion, bionic implants are a grand testament to human innovation and our abilities to push beyond the natural limits. As we tread forward in this Cyborg age, the intersection of technology and humanity continues to unravel tremendous potential in improving lives and health prospects. Beyond the physical, it initiates dialogue on fundamental questions about our identity and humanity. While technology integration brings unparalleled opportunities, we must ponder the ethical, social, and psychological impacts of this development.

Far beyond a mere fusion of flesh and technology, we stand on the precipice of a new age - an age where humans and machines become ever more closely intertwined, paving the path towards a future limited only by our imagination and our will to venture into the unknown. In the inevitable Cyborg Age, we enter an era of ever-greater complexity but also one of exhilarating possibilities.

# Chapter 5. Real-life Cyborgs: Stories of Transformation

The integration of biology and technology has seen impressive strides in recent times, no less notable in the creation of extraordinary bionic implants. We have seen real-life cyborgs emerge from among everyday people who embrace these technologies, yielding significant improvements in quality of life. From a finger that doubles as a USB drive to artificial limbs with advanced sensory-input capabilities, these breakthroughs have had transformative consequences.

## 5.1. The Trailblazer – Neil Harbisson

At the forefront of the cyborg revolution, our first stop finds us with Neil Harbisson, a color-blind artist from the United Kingdom. Born with achromatopsia, a severe form of color blindness that sees the world only in grayscale, Harbisson chose to perceive the world through a different spectrum.

Just imagine a slender, flexible rod arching over the top of Neil's head, one end fastened neatly into his skull while the other hovers just above his eyebrows like an antenna. This is his "eyeborg," essentially a camera capturing colors around him and transforming them into vibrations that he perceives as sound. To him, red might be a low note, blue a high one. Over time, he's trained his brain to recognize and understand these auditory representations of color. Furthermore, the eyeborg enables him to detect infrared and ultraviolet, frequencies far beyond human perception. Harbisson has altered his reality, making the imperceptible perceivable.

## 5.2. The Power of Touch – Claudia Mitchell

As we navigate further into the realm of transformative bionic technology, we meet Claudia Mitchell, a former U.S Marine, who lost her left arm in a motorcycle accident. Determined not to let her amputation stand in the way of her daily life, she agreed to participate in an experimental procedure designed to install a bionic arm that can respond to her thoughts.

Developed by the Johns Hopkins Applied Physics Lab, the Modular Prosthetic Limb (MPL) is an engineering marvel. Coupled with a revolutionary procedure called Target Muscle Reinnervation, Claudia's chest muscles were rewired to receive the electrical signals sent by her brain to move her non-existing limb. These signals are picked up by sensors and sent to the MPL, which interprets them and moves accordingly.

Most impressively, the MPL can recreate a limited sense of touch. When someone or something applies pressure, sensors in the MPL's fingertips send signals back to Claudia's chest, where she can perceive the sensation. Even though her arm is missing, Mitchell hasn't lost her ability to reach out and touch the world.

## 5.3. Man and Machine in Harmony – Hugh Herr

Our excursion takes us next to Hugh Herr, who, after a mountaineering accident at the age of 17, had both his legs amputated. Refusing to be held back, Herr devoted his life to making better prostheses. Today, he heads the Biomechatronics Research Group at MIT Media Lab, spearheading research in electromechanical prosthetics and other bio-interactive machines.

Herr's personal bionic legs are no ordinary prostheses. Crafted using cybernetics and AI, his legs adapt to different terrains automatically, actively learning his gait and movement patterns for optimal performance. With built-in sensors and microprocessors, they adjust strength and speed, providing a natural feel.

In 2014, Herr demonstrated his bionic limbs by climbing the stage of a TED conference unassisted, a testament to the advanced state of his life's work. Herr's ability to stride onto that stage showcased how machine learning and robotics can work together to create truly transformative bionic technology.

# 5.4. The Bionic Visionary – Jens Naumann

Finally, we introduce Jens Naumann. Having lost his vision in both eyes, Naumann became involved in an experimental procedure that promised him a second chance at sight. The procedure involved implanting a chip into his visual cortex and connecting it to a low-resolution camera mounted on a pair of glasses.

Naumann described the bionic vision as very different from natural human vision, more like a stream of black and white points, dots moving with the outline of the object. But that didn't detract from its magnitude. Many people who are blind would give a lot to experience that, to see silhouette and motion, and generally sense the world visually, making Naumann's transformation a particularly moving one.

These stories of transformation are but a few glimpses of the power of bionic implants, capturing the essence of this revolutionary intersection of biology, technology, and the indomitable human spirit. The rise of the Cyborg Age is more than just science fiction unfolding before our eyes; it's a testament to our capacity to reimagine our potential, question our limitations, and strive to improve the human condition.

# Chapter 6. Bionic Implants: The Medical Breakthroughs

A quantum leap in the field of medicine has been accomplished through the development and application of bionic implants, fundamentally altering the landscape of healthcare and heralding an unprecedented era of medical breakthroughs. The unwavering, relentless progress of technology elucidated through bionic implants spills into every aspect of medicine - from restoring lost bodily functions to augmenting natural human abilities. In the following pages, we shall trek the journey of bionic implants, dissecting the science, innovations, concerns, and future possibilities, promising a comprehensive trek into this awe-inspiring medical realm.

## 6.1. The Science Behind The Miracle

Bionic implants are a culmination of biology, engineering, materials science, and computing - an interdisciplinary field forming the bedrock of bioinformatics. At their core, bionic implants are electronic-prosthetic devices that can replace or augment organs or parts of the human body. They interface directly with the nervous system, facilitating a two-way conversation between the device and the brain. This ground-breaking achievement, carried on the back of technological evolution, leverages the principles of neuroplasticity, the brain's ability to reorganize itself by forming new neural connections.

Sensors in these implants translate biological signals such as nerve impulses into digital language that a computer can comprehend. Vice versa, digital information can be converted to dynamic, biologically compatible signals that our nerves understand. This symbiotic translation from biological to digital (and vice versa) has unlocked doors hitherto unimaginable in medical practice.

## 6.2. From Conception to Realization

The journey of developing a bionic implant is marked with challenges - both technical and ethical. Broaching uncharted territory, scientists undergo rigorous experimentation, trial periods, multiple iterations, and thorough peer reviews before an implant is deemed ready for market application.

Materials used in implants need to be biocompatible to prevent rejection by the host body. Silicon, titanium, ceramics, and medical-grade polymers are commonly used. Implants also need to withstand the harsh environment within the human body: varying pH levels, body fluids, and rigorous mechanical stress. Powering such devices efficiently, safely, and in a compact fashion is another feat, often addressed by wireless charging techniques or energy-harvesting methods from the body's heat or movement.

## 6.3. A Panacea for the Sensory Impaired

Bionic implants have been hailed as a panacea for the sensory impaired. Cochlear implants, for example, have transformed the lives of the hearing-impaired by bypassing damaged parts of the auditory system and directly stimulating the auditory nerve. For people who are visually impaired or blind, retinal implants, a still-developing technology, aim to restore partial vision by transmitting visual information from a camera directly to the brain.

## 6.4. Lifelines for the Heart and Beyond

While their use in sensory augmentations is certainly noteworthy, the bionic realm's scope is much more expansive. One of the oldest and most successful bionic implants, the artificial cardiac pacemaker, monitors and controls the heartbeat, sending electrical impulses to the heart muscle to maintain an adequate heart rate. Ventricular assist devices, though not entirely bionic, assist a heart that's weak or failing, buying precious time before a heart transplant can take place.

In recent years, brain implants have come to the foreground. For instance, deep brain stimulation, where implanted electrodes send electric pulses to specific parts of the brain, has shown success in managing Parkinson's disease and other neurological conditions.

## 6.5. Ethical Considerations and Controversies

As with any transformative technology, ethical paradigms must be revisited and revised. Concerns about the potential misuse of bionic technologies, particularly in non-therapeutic, 'enhancement' applications, are a hotly debated topic. A form of biological 'hack', these improvements could challenge and complicate the definition of what it means to be human. It is crucial that thorough ethical discussions and regulations accompany the advancement of bionic technology.

## 6.6. The Road Ahead

The future of bionic implants, brimming with potential, beckons a bright era in healthcare, possibly expanding beyond it to reshape human existence. Enhanced cognition, superhuman strength, or heightened senses through augmentation - these are no longer the fodder of science fiction, but an impending reality. The day isn't far when we'll truly wear our hearts on our sleeves and our brains in our hands.

In the end, the primary aim remains to improve the quality of life, whether through restoration or augmentation. As we stand at the precipice of the Cyborg Age, we must remember that technical advancements combined with a compassionate, ethical approach will yield the real fruits of this exciting phase of our technological evolution.

# Chapter 7. Ethics in the Cyborg Age: Balancing Progress and Principles

As we straddle the convergence point of human biology and ever-advancing technology, we encounter an array of complex ethical dilemmas. These question our moral principles around the nature of humanity, individuality, fairness, and the socio-economic implications that the transformative era of the Cyborg Age presents. The delicate balancing act between the invaluable advancements of bionic augmentation and the principles that maintain our societal fabric forms a crux of this discourse.

## 7.1. Disruption of Human Identity

The idea of integrating technology into the human body challenges our conventional understanding of human nature. Should we view bionic augmentation merely as an enhancement of the human body, or a violation of natural boundary? Furthermore, if individuals integrate AI into their cognitive processes, it could blur the lines between behavior and programming, raising questions about free will and responsibility.

We must also consider the question of how we value and understand humanity if there are significant numbers of significantly augmented humans. From a societal perspective, do we appreciate humans and cyborgs on an equal footing, or will biases emerge? This challenge necessitates an ongoing dialogue that should inspire a collective reevaluation of our definition of humanity, and a renewal of ethics that can accommodate this new paradigm.

## 7.2. The Fair Access Dilemma

The democratization of technology is crucial to maintain social equilibrium in the Cyborg Age. If bionic enhancements are prohibitively expensive and only accessible to the wealthy, it could lead to a sharp increase in social disparity. Those who can afford these enhancements will invariably have an edge in various facets of life, resulting in a socio-economic chasm.

As much as we must strive to advance technology, we need to simultaneously strive for inclusive policies and frameworks that democratize access to these technologies ensuring nobody is left behind in this cybernetic revolution. Doing so will require cooperative strategic actions from stakeholders, including governments, scientists, ethicists, policy-makers, and civil society groups.

## 7.3. The Autonomy and Consent

Debates about autonomy and consent will become increasingly crucial as we further explore brain augmentation and cognitive enhancement. If an individual is unable to provide informed consent due to cognitive impairment, who should make decisions about their possible enhancement? Additionally, as implants become more advanced, there'll be an even more pivotal question about how much influence these devices could have over an individual's behavior or cognition. Thus, the right to autonomy and comprehensive understanding of consent procedures need to be at the forefront of any bio-tech legislation.

## 7.4. Regulatory Frameworks and Oversight

Creating robust and comprehensive regulatory frameworks for

bionic technologies is another complex ethical consideration. To protect individual rights, prevent misuse, and ensure the welfare of society at large, these frameworks require meticulously detailed legislation. However, they also must be flexible enough to accommodate rapid technological advancements without stifling innovation.

In tandem with a robust legal framework, an international body will be needed to monitor the enforcement of these laws, maintain their relevance as technology progresses, and uphold ethical standards. The inclusion of ethicists into scientific research projects at the earliest stages would be another proactive step towards integrating cutting-edge technology within an ethical framework.

# 7.5. The Alteration of Physical Capabilities

Our traditional understanding of physical capability, disability, competition, and fairness could be fundamentally altered in the Cyborg Age. With bionic limbs that can potentially outperform their biological counterparts, what would this mean for professional sports? Would it be fair for surgically enhanced individuals to compete alongside unenhanced individuals? Similarly, if bionic enhancement becomes mainstream, will our perception of "disability" transform?

This subchapter calls for a careful reevaluation and adaptation of our moral, legal, and societal judgments regarding physical capabilities and disabilities. It invites us to rethink the principles of fairness, in light of our new possibilities.

In summary, technological advancements in the realm of bionic implants raise several ethical considerations that require thoughtful discussion and deliberate action. Bridging humanity with cyborg capabilities pushes us to adapt our principles flexibly, without undermining the core values that define our societal structure. Ultimately, the Cyborg Age poses a challenge that is as philosophical as it is technological, pressing us to strike a delicate balance between progress and principles. The intensity and complexity of these ethical questions only underscore the significance of the Cyborg Age as a defining moment in human history. Thus, we must rise to meet this future with open dialogue, inclusive policies, and heightened moral consciousness – embracing this epoch-making transition with both excitement and responsibility.

# Chapter 8. Technological Advances Fuelling the Cyborg Revolution

It's evident that the enthralling reality of human cyborgs we see in movies and read about in novels is no longer a mere flight of fantasy. The advent of breakthrough technological advances is spurring this riveting change to become a tangible existence, powering the inception and exponential development of the Cyborg Age.

Scientific progress in various disciplines, encompassing material science, robotics, biomedical engineering, nano-biology, AI, and computer science, is converging towards designing and constructing devices that go beyond conventional prosthetics and medical implants. These bionic devices intertwine so seamlessly within human anatomy and physiology that they are becoming a part of us, enhancing our abilities while restoring, and sometimes surpassing, natural bodily functions.

## 8.1. The Contribution of Material Science and Robotics

Material Science and Robotics stand as the pillars of the cyborg revolution. Material Scientists have demonstrated the capability to develop biocompatible materials that are not rejected by our bodies, but rather integrate freely with our biological systems. These materials, like titanium alloys and biologically inert polymers, mirror the properties of body tissues, enabling the perfect fit within the human form.

Similarly, the world of robotics offers tantalising possibilities. Mimicking human movements, designs termed as 'biomimetic' allow for sophisticated bionic limbs. They enable more organic movements by closely imitating the natural kinematics and dynamics of our bodies. These biomechanical marvels powered by myoelectric signals from residual muscles allow the amputees and those with paralysis to regain mobility, touch, and sensation, ushering in newfound freedom and autonomy.

## 8.2. Biomedical Engineering and Nano-Biology

Biomedical engineering is at the forefront of blending biology and engineering, creating bionic devices tailored for individual necessities. This field has given rise to cochlear implants, restoring a sense of sound to the deaf, retinal implants to endow vision to the blind, and even bionic pancreases that can regulate insulin for diabetics.

Nano-biology has been essential in promoting the growth of neural interface technology—an integral field for the development of advanced bionic implants. Here, nanoparticles play a crucial role in nerve regeneration and the creation of neural pathways for bionic devices, effectively linking the device to the brain at a microscopic level.

## 8.3. AI and Computer Science

The intersection of AI and computer science has significantly contributed to making bionic implants smarter and more intuitive than ever. Machine Learning methods help in decoding neural signals, transforming them into movements for bionic limbs. This results in fluid and lifelike movements that elude the mechanical stiffness often associated with artificial limbs.

AI also enables real-time adaptation in bionic devices. Sensors embedded within these devices gather data relative to the user and the environment, helping the device 'learn' and 'adapt' user-specific behaviors.

## 8.4. Sensory Substitution and Augmentation Tools

Apart from replacing lost functions, pioneering advances are also channeling efforts to augment the human sensory system. Through neurofeedback systems coupled with bionic technology, the bounds of human perception are being tested, and new sensorial experiences are being created.

Sound is converted to sight for the visually impaired, magnetic fields are perceived as tangible sensations, and infrared vision is no longer a superhuman trait. We are witnessing an exciting era where senses are not just being restored but also invented.

At the microscopic level, micro and nano bots promise an exhilarating expectation of a future where these tiny robots could swim through our bloodstreams, monitoring health and repairing damage at the cellular level.

## 8.5. The Implications and Ethical Considerations

The continued progression towards the Cyborg Age is not without its caveats. Deciphering and mitigating potential risks arising from our increasing symbiosis with machines remains a daunting challenge. Questions related to privacy, control, security, and disparities in access must be conscientiously addressed as we tread forward in our technological renaissance.

As we march towards the Cyborg Age, the journey promises to be as incredible as the future we are striving towards. As advancements continue to oscillate between enhancing human capabilities and redesigning human experiences, we reiterate the multidimensional transformation ushered in by the bionic revolution.

As the boundaries between man and machine continue to blur, we are on the precipice of creating a new species entirely - Homo Technologicus, propelled by the relentless vigor of technological innovation. The realization of the Cyborg Age progressively alters our worldview, intensifying the discourse on what it means to be human, as we persist in the daring adventure of creating a harmonious union between humanity and machinery.

# Chapter 9. The Economic Impact of Bionic Implants

A renaissance of sorts is currently unfolding in the global healthcare sector. An age where bionic implants are no longer reserved for the pages of sci-fi novels or silver screens, but are shaping real-world narratives, bringing about radical transformations in individuals' lives and promising profound transformations to the economic landscape to boot.

## 9.1. The Burden of Disability

Let's commence by considering the current standing of disability: to see the growing problem that the world grapples with and where bionic technology intervenes. The World Health Organization (WHO) noted in 2021 that over a billion people, or about 15% of global population, live with some form of disability. This is a substantial portion of humanity that is directly affected.

Moreover, the costs associated with disabilities are multi-faceted and significant. These include direct medical costs such as physician visits, medications, hospital stays, surgeries, and physical therapies, as well as indirect expenditures resulting from productivity losses, such as reduced work hours, absenteeism, and premature death. By adopting bionic technology, not only can we mitigate the physical and psychological ramifications for the individuals affected, but we can also exert a significant economic advantage by alleviating these associated costs.

# 9.2. Bionic Technology: A Healthcare Game-changer

Bionic implants represent a revolution in treatment possibilities. They are unique in that they meld the human body with sophisticated technology to produce some semblance of a normal life for those afflicted by various forms of disabilities.

Bionic eye implants, for instance, are becoming increasingly advanced, offering hope to individuals affected by vision loss. Cochlear implants allow those with profound hearing loss the chance to hear again. Prosthetics have evolved from simple mechanical apparatus to complex bionic limbs that provide functionality closer to natural limbs. Bionic organs like artificial pancreases and hearts can radically improve the survival rates and quality of life for those with severe organ diseases.

This level of technological advancement in the healthcare sector denotes two major economic implications. The first is the direct economic contribution in terms of market size and jobs this budding industry can create. The second is through savings from reduced healthcare and disability-related costs.

# 9.3. The Economic Footprint of the Bionic Industry

Globally, the bionics market was valued at approximately $18.5 billion in 2020 and is projected to reach nearly $31.5 billion by 2027, growing at a compound annual growth rate (CAGR) of roughly 7.5% during the forecast period 2021-2027.

The bionics industry isn't just about the manufacturers who design and produce these implants, there are also service sectors like tune-up and repair workshops, training centres for usage, and the R&D

institutions that contribute to the continual development of these technologies.

Moreover, the industry is a hotbed for high-skilled employment. From biotechnologists, biomedical engineers, to medical health professionals specialising in the installation and use of these devices, the bionic industry is poised to be a key job creator in the new tech-dominated economy.

## 9.4. Healthcare Cost Reductions and Quality of Life Enhancements

To comprehend the cost-saving aspects, we need to consider two primary categories: Direct and Indirect savings. Direct savings accumulate from the reduction of extended healthcare service use, including lengthy hospital stays, repetitive surgeries, medications, and lifelong therapies. Indirect savings come from increased workforce participation and productivity, reducing the cost burden on society and increasing Gross Domestic Product (GDP).

Bionic implants can also dramatically enhance quality of life for the affected individuals, allowing them to live independently and engage more thoroughly in society, which leads to enhanced mental well-being.

In the larger picture, a more inclusive society, represented by the maximized participation of people who previously couldn't contribute actively due to physical impairments, will further enrich the socio-cultural fabric and stability of societies.

## 9.5. Investments, Innovations, and Infrastructure

Expanding the bionics sector will require substantial investment to propel innovation and build the appropriate supporting infrastructure. This includes investing in education to train the next generation of scientists, engineers, and technicians who will propel this field forward.

Such investments can spur on economic growth and play a significant role in reshaping public perspectives towards disability and technological integration with the human body. Moreover, they also contribute to the social imperative of inclusivity, propelling us further towards a balanced society.

## 9.6. The Road Ahead

Clearly, the potential economic impact surrounding bionic implants is significant, marked by a combination of increased market size, job creation, health care savings, and improved quality of life. Nevertheless, much work lies ahead. Besides the technological hurdles, the ethical, legal and social concerns surrounding bionic implants present considerable challenges that society must address moving forward.

As we venture further into this brave new world, the belief that the integration of biological and technological realms can create a more inclusive and productive society seems increasingly justified. Quite possibly, the bionic age will revolutionize our socio-economic landscape, just as the age of personal computing and the internet did. In the grand scheme of things, bionic implants won't just change lives; they will reshape the contours of our society and economy.

# Chapter 10. Societal Changes in the Cyborg Age

Since the dawn of civilization, every epochal shift in technological advancements has reverberated through societies, shaping and molding our ways of life in ways unanticipated, complex, and profound. The Cyborg Age, where humans start to merge with machines through bionic implants and enhancements, is a transformative era that's no exception.

## 10.1. Social Relationships and Bionics

As we begin to fathom the societal transformations influenced by the integration of bionic technology, one cannot overlook the implications on our interpersonal relationships. The augmentation of our physical abilities through bionics can unlock an unprecedented level of communication possibilities. For instance, a chip implant allowing the control of digital devices, combined with advances in augmented and virtual reality, could enable the creation of deeply immersive communication platforms. These platforms would lend communication more lived and tangible, molding social relationships in ways we have just begun to imagine.

Similarly, health tracking implants could provide loved ones with real-time health data, enabling an extraordinary level of care and nurturing in relationships. However, it will also pose significant ethical questions around privacy and consent which societies will have to navigate delicately.

## 10.2. The Concept of Disability and Cybernetics

The frontier where the Cyborg Age can arguably have the most profound impact is in redefining our understanding and attitudes towards disabilities. Traditionally viewed through a lens of limitation, disability in the Cyborg Age could be transformed into a canvas for human enhancement. Imagine a world where artificial limbs do not just restore mobility but enhance it, catalyzing superhuman agility; or cochlear implants that not only rectify hearing impairments, but also discern frequencies beyond the typical human range.

This fundamentally changes the societal discourse around disabilities, moving it from a narrative of "coping" and "managing" to one of "enhancement" and "surpassing". It also necessitates a robust and inclusive legal and social framework to ensure fair and equitable access to these augmentations and guard against potential misuse.

## 10.3. Bionics and the Workplace

In the realm of employment and professional life, the Cyborg Age holds equal promise and challenges. On one hand, the augmentation of physical and cognitive capabilities could lead to significant productivity boosts and new forms of labor. For instance, bionic implants to enhance memory, computation, or physical strength could radically redefine the nature of various professions.

Simultaneously, these enhancements risk widening the socio-economic disparities, as those who can afford the augmentations might gain an unfair advantage in the competitive job market. This potential 'cybernetic divide' would have profound implications, necessitating the already pressing debate around legislations and restrictions to ensure a fair and equitable transition to this new era.

# 10.4. Ethical and Legal Considerations

While these transformations and their societal impacts are undoubtedly fascinating, they also raise deep ethical, legal, and philosophical questions. We will have to interrogate the balance between human enhancement and dehumanization, and consider who gets to define these boundaries.

Moreover, it would require intensive deliberation around issues of cognitive liberty, body autonomy, and the ethical use of these implants. Regulations and laws will unsurprisingly be forced to evolve, keeping pace with these dizzying advancements to ensure that the sanctity of human rights is upheld even as we traverse into this new, promising, yet undeniably complex era.

# 10.5. Conclusion

As we stand on this frontier, bionic implants and the resultant Cyborg Age offer us the opportunity to redefine our societal structures in ways that lean towards inclusivity, adaptability, and enhancement. At the same time, these changes call for an acute awareness of the critical ethical and justice-related issues that need to be addressed.

In this intricate dance between possibilities and challenges, our collective responsibility extends beyond embracing these advancements - it also lies in steering them for the equitable, ethical, and sustainable transformation of our societies. In the optimistic vision of the Cyborg Age's societal changes, lays the potential blueprint for a just, inclusive, and bold new world.

The journey into this anticipated era, though fraught with challenges, is an exciting vista of opportunities pushing the boundaries of human potential. As we continue the exploration, the Cyborg Age calls us to partake in the driving seat, shaping technology to augment our societies, rather than letting it dictate the course of our evolution.

# Chapter 11. The Future: Predictions and Possibilities in the Bionic Era

As we stand on the brink of the Bionic Era, we occupy an unusual position, somewhere between awestruck wonder at the possibilities before us, and curious apprehension about the unknowns yet to be confronted in a world where humans and machines become increasingly integrated. This juncture in time opens up myriad questions about what comes next: how will our lives be shaped, transformed, or even enriched by bionic technologies? While it is impossible to predict the future with perfect accuracy, there are a few key trends and developments we can expect to see. Let us delve into these predictions and possibilities.

## 11.1. A Shift in Medical Landscape

The first, and perhaps most profound, change we can expect to see will be a massive shift in the medical landscape. Bionic technologies will revolutionize the way we think about, diagnose, and treat a myriad of conditions, considerably augmenting our capabilities and providing new hope for genetic diseases, disabilities, or injuries.

Medical fields such as orthopedics, cardiology, neurology, and even psychology stand to benefit enormously from bionic advancements. Devices like cochlear implants and retinal prostheses have already demonstrated the ability to restore or replace senses once thought to be irrevocably lost. In the future, we could anticipate even more ambitious accomplishments, such as bionic hearts for cardiovascular patients or neural prostheses to address paralysis or dystrophy. Pain management may also see a new dawn with the evolution of smart bionic system that trace and neutralize pain signals before they reach the brain.

# 11.2. Augmentation Beyond Medicinal Purposes

While the medical field is the first to come to mind when one thinks of bionics, the scope of these technologies extends far beyond health and disease. Human augmentation, the practice of using technology to enhance our innate capabilities, looks set to profoundly reshape not only our capabilities as individuals, but society as a whole.

In our day-to-day lives, wearables and other augmentation technologies might blur the line between the physical and digital worlds, taking today's smartphone functionality and integrating it into our bodies. Devices to improve memory or cognitive processing speed may become as common as glasses or contact lenses are today. Digital connectivity could become a literal part of us, with implants providing real-time access to information, personal data, and communication tools right at the neural level.

It's reasonable to assume that the convergence of bionics and other technologies like AI and VR/AR will further revolutionize our personal and professional domains. Remote collaboration may transcend to another level with the use of bionic interfaces, making the physical environment irrelevant for many tasks.

# 11.3. The Prosthetics Revolution

While bionic prosthetics have already proven their life-changing potential, the future holds even more promise. As bionics technologies continue to advance, we can expect to see prosthetics that are not merely functional replacements but are essentially superhuman. Enhanced strength, speed, and endurance could become a reality with devices of this nature, altering the field of competitive sports and manual labor.

Mind-controlled prosthetics may soon be a common sight, further blurring the boundary between the biological and the artificial. Mundane tasks such as lifting, walking, or even running could be dramatically augmented, making life easier and drastically improving the quality of living for those in need.

## 11.4. Ethical and Social Challenges Ahead

While the dramatic possibilities associated with bionic tech inspire awe, they also bring considerable ethical and social conundrums into sharp focus. As remarkable as the potential benefits are, careful thought must be given to the societal impact of such technologies.

While we aim to improve quality of life and abilities, we may also grapple with the issues of inequality. Not everyone may have equal access to these benefits due to economic disparity, in a society where bionic enhancement is a reality. This could create a "bionic divide," between those who can afford enhancements and those who cannot, further increasing socioeconomic inequality.

Additionally, issues around security and privacy, particularly concerning data that is collected and transmitted via implants, are also key factors that need strong policy framework. Attention to these concerns will be paramount to foster an environment supportive of bionic advancements, while maintaining the trust and security of individuals and societies.

## 11.5. Embracing the Promise of Bionics

Despite the challenges that lay ahead, at the heart of the bionic age is a profound promise: to transcend the limitations of our biological bodies, and to open up a world of possibilities hitherto unseen in human history. From a rehabilitative perspective, opening the door to a life once imagined to be lost, to an augmentative perspective, boosting our intrinsic sensory, cognitive, or physical capabilities, these bionic breakthroughs hold the potential to redefine every domain of human life.

As we journey into the future of the Bionic Era, societal conversation, progressive policy-making, research, innovation, and most importantly, accepting the change is critically needed to responsibly navigate this new frontier. It promises to be quite a journey – an exploratory venture filled with optimism, excitement, and ushering in a new age for mankind.